ANIMAL KINGDOM CLASSIFICATION

BATS, BLUE WHALES & OTHER
MAMMALS

BY STEVE PARKER
CONTENT ADVISER: ROBERT M. TIMM, PH.D., CURATOR OF
MAMMALS, MUSEUM OF NATURAL HISTORY, UNIVERSITY OF KANSAS

SCIENCE ADVISER: TERRENCE E. YOUNG JR., M.ED., M.L.S.,
JEFFERSON PARISH (LOUISIANA) PUBLIC SCHOOL SYSTEM

First published in the United States in 2006 by
Compass Point Books
3109 West 50th St., #115
Minneapolis, MN 55410

ANIMAL KINGDOM CLASSIFICATION–MAMMALS
was produced by

David West Children's Books
7 Princeton Court
55 Felsham Road
London SW15 1AZ

Designer: David West
Editors: Gail Bushnell, Nadia Higgins, Kate Newport
Page Production: Les Tranby, James Mackey

Visit Compass Point Books on the Internet at
www.compasspointbooks.com
or e-mail your request to
custserv@compasspointbooks.com

Library of Congress Cataloging-in-Publication Data
Parker, Steve.
   Bats, blue whales, and other mammals /
   by Steve Parker.
      p. cm. — (Animal kingdom classification)
   Includes bibliographical references (p.   ) and index.
   ISBN 0-7565-1253-0 (hard cover)
   1. Mammals—Juvenile literature. I. Title. II. Series.
   QL706.2.B363 2005
   599—dc22

PHOTO CREDITS :
Abbreviations: t-top, m-middle, b-bottom, r-right,
l-left, c-center.

9br, Doc White/naturepl.com; 9br(inset), Dietmar Nill/naturepl.com; 12bl, Rod Williams/naturepl.com; 13br, naturepl.com; 15tl, Pete Oxford/naturepl.com; 17b(inset), Captain Budd Christman, NOAA Corps; 18t, Hans Christoph Kappel/naturepl.com; 19tl & mr, Bruce Davidson/naturepl.com; 19b, Dave Watts/naturepl.com; 20t, Tim Macmillan/John Downer pr/naturepl.com; 21t, John Waters/naturepl.com; 21m, Anup Shah/naturepl.com; 21br, naturepl.com; 22-23 & 36t, OAR National Undersea Research Program (NURP), University of North Carolina at Wilmington; 23bl, OAR National Undersea Research Program (NURP), National Maritime Lab; 22br, Captain Budd Christman, NOAA Corps; 23tr, Dr. James P. McVey, NOAA Sea Grant Program; 23mr & br, naturepl.com; 24bm, naturepl.com; 25tm, Peter Blackwell/naturepl.com; 25tr, Francois Savigny/naturepl.com; 25br, naturepl.com; 26t, Peter Blackwell/naturepl.com; 27br, naturepl.com; 28br, Bruce Davidson/naturepl.com; 29m, Brian Lightfoot/naturepl.com; 29bl,Tero Niemi/Naturbild/naturepl.com; 29br, naturepl.com; 31br, Nick Garbutt/naturepl.com; 32-33, Peter Blackwell/naturepl.com; 33mr, Captain Budd Christman, NOAA Corps; 33bl, David Tipling/naturepl.com; 33br, naturepl.com; 35tl, Jeff Foot/naturepl.com; 35tr, Heikki Willamo/Naturbild/naturepl.com; 35b, naturepl.com; 36bl, naturepl.com; 36br, Peter Basset/naturepl.com; 37t, Dave Watts/naturepl.com; 38 inset, Captain Budd Christman, NOAA Corps; 38bl,Klaus Echle/naturepl.com; 39tr, T.J. Rich/naturepl.com; 39bl, naturepl.com; 41tl & br, Dave Watts/naturepl.com; 41tr, naturepl.com; 42bl, Michael Pitts/naturepl.com; 43tl, John Cancalosi/naturepl.com; 43br, Fabio Liverani/naturepl.com; 45b, Digital Vision.

Every effort has been made to contact copyright holders of any material reproduced in this book. Any omissions will be rectified in subsequent printings if notice is given to the publishers.

Front cover: Grizzly bear
Opposite: Mandrill

ANIMAL KINGDOM CLASSIFICATION

BATS, BLUE WHALES & OTHER
MAMMALS

Steve Parker

COMPASS POINT BOOKS MINNEAPOLIS, MINNESOTA

TABLE OF CONTENTS

INTRODUCTION

Most of the animals we see every day are mammals. Pets such as rabbits and gerbils belong to this group, as do farm animals including cows and sheep. Powerful racehorses, pesky rats, and our furry friends—dogs and cats—are all mammals that share our daily lives. However, most mammals are much less common than these. We may be lucky enough to see some of the more rare mammals, such as tigers in Asian jungles, elephants on the African plains, and whales in the oceans. But others are far more obscure, such as solenodons, linsangs, and babirusas.

The types of mammals we know about depend a lot on where we live. Different mammals are familiar to people in different places. No matter where they live, however, humans seem drawn to mammals. They are also warm-blooded, often active, good at learning, and have fur or hair—just like us. This is because we are mammals, too.

CHARGING TIGER

Most of us recognize one of the best-known mammals. Yet it is also one of the rarest. There are only a few thousand tigers left. And the largest, the Siberian tiger (right), is the rarest of all, with just a few hundred surviving. Most people view the tiger as a beautiful big cat. Others see it as money—they kill it and sell its body parts.

WORLD OF MAMMALS

F ew parts of planet Earth are mammal-free—only the most frozen parts of the far north and south. Over 4,500 species of mammals can be found in every other habitat.

LAND HABITATS

Most mammals are land-dwellers. Among the harshest terrestrial habitats is the semi-frozen, treeless tundra of the far north. Yet musk ox, caribou, lemmings, and arctic foxes and hares survive here. The wind, ice, and snow of high mountains are too much of a challenge for most creatures. But mammals like bighorn sheep, yak, and snow leopards endure the conditions. Lack of water means a tough life, too. Even so, kit foxes, kangaroos, and camels cope in various deserts across the world.

Warmth and moisture encourage all kinds of life, including plants to eat. So most types of mammals are found in woods and forests. In particular, the steamy tropical rain forests are home to about half of all kinds of mammals.

SEAS AND SKIES

Although most mammals stay on dry land, others have conquered our planet's largest habitat—the open ocean. Whales, dolphins, porpoises, seals, and sea lions are all perfectly adapted to life among the waves. Even in the air, mammals thrive. Some are gliders and swoopers, such as "flying" squirrels. But bats are true masters of the air, and they make up about one-fourth of all kinds of mammals.

DESERTS
Kit foxes

GRASSLANDS
Giraffes

TROPICAL FORESTS
Tiger

RIVERS AND LAKES
Hippopotamus

NORTHERN FORESTS
Tree porcupine

MOUNTAINS
Bighorn sheep

TEMPERATE FORESTS
Koala bear

POLAR REGIONS
Harp seal pup

OCEANS
Killer whale (orca)

BIGGEST AND SMALLEST

No other group of animals includes such a wide range of sizes. The biggest mammal of all is the blue whale at 98 feet (29.8 meters) and weighing more than 100 tons (90 metric tons). One of the smallest is the hog-nosed bat. It's smaller than your thumb and weighs just over half an ounce (2 grams). That's 50 million times less than the blue whale! Most mammals are in the smaller size range, between mice and rabbits.

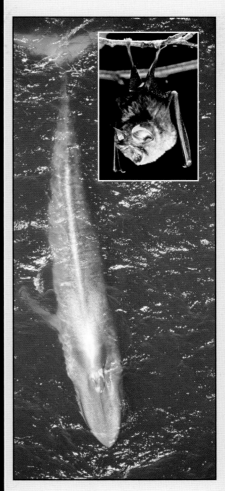

Blue whale
Inset: Kitti's hog-nosed bat

MAMMAL BODIES

Mammals belong to the main animal group known as vertebrates. Their skeletons include a spinal column made of backbones called vertebrae. Other characteristics include warm blood, fur or hair, and the ability to nurse their young with mother's milk.

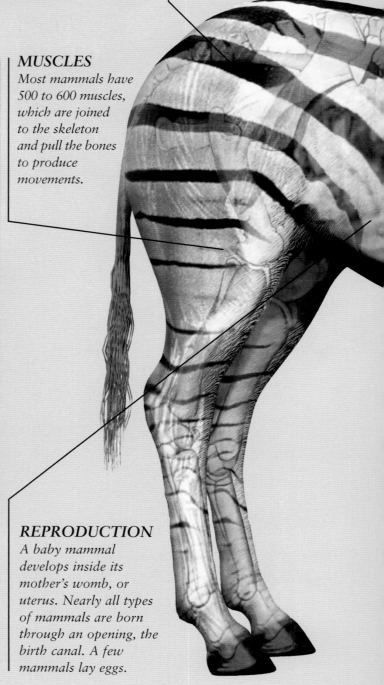

SKIN AND HAIR OR FUR

Hair or fur grows from tiny follicles in the skin. Sweat glands produce sweat that keeps body temperature stable in very hot conditions.

WARM BLOOD

Only two groups of animals are warm-blooded—mammals and birds. Warm-blooded means the body is kept at the same warm temperature at all times, even when the surroundings are freezing. This means mammals can be active in ice and snow, when cold-blooded animals like snakes and insects are too cold to move.

MUSCLES

Most mammals have 500 to 600 muscles, which are joined to the skeleton and pull the bones to produce movements.

NURSING YOUNG

A mammal mother's milk is made in mammary glands, located on her front or underside. (This is where the name mammal comes from.) The young suckle, or feed on this milk, for their first days and weeks. The milk contains all they need to grow and stay healthy.

REPRODUCTION

A baby mammal develops inside its mother's womb, or uterus. Nearly all types of mammals are born through an opening, the birth canal. A few mammals lay eggs.

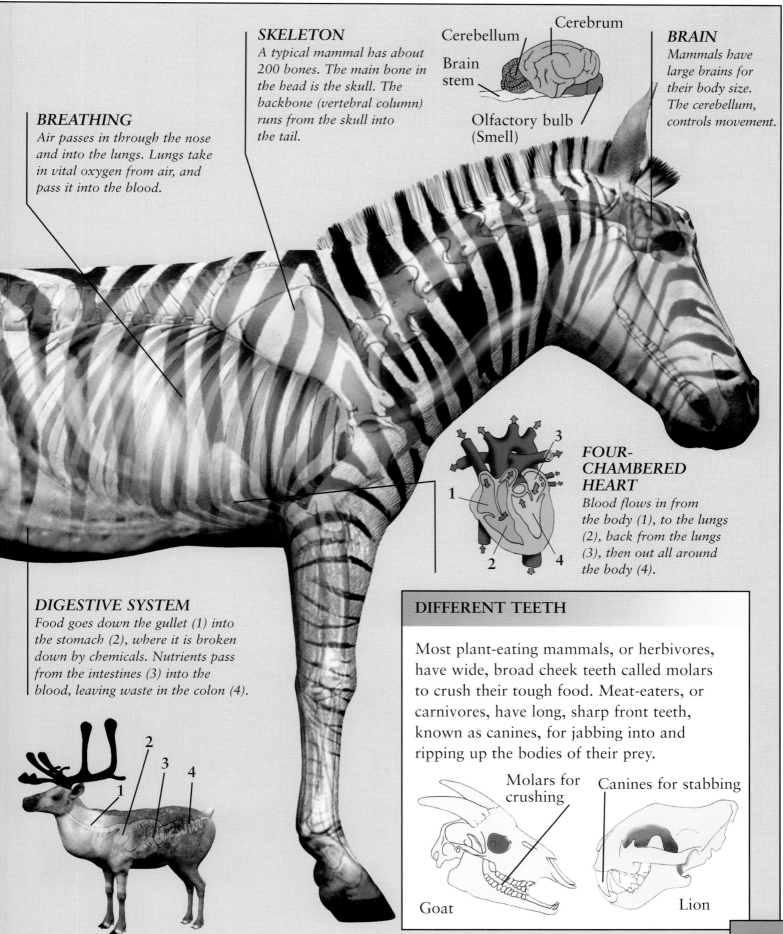

BREATHING

Air passes in through the nose and into the lungs. Lungs take in vital oxygen from air, and pass it into the blood.

SKELETON

A typical mammal has about 200 bones. The main bone in the head is the skull. The backbone (vertebral column) runs from the skull into the tail.

Cerebellum

Cerebrum

Brain stem

Olfactory bulb (Smell)

BRAIN

Mammals have large brains for their body size. The cerebellum, controls movement.

FOUR-CHAMBERED HEART

Blood flows in from the body (1), to the lungs (2), back from the lungs (3), then out all around the body (4).

DIGESTIVE SYSTEM

Food goes down the gullet (1) into the stomach (2), where it is broken down by chemicals. Nutrients pass from the intestines (3) into the blood, leaving waste in the colon (4).

DIFFERENT TEETH

Most plant-eating mammals, or herbivores, have wide, broad cheek teeth called molars to crush their tough food. Meat-eaters, or carnivores, have long, sharp front teeth, known as canines, for jabbing into and ripping up the bodies of their prey.

Molars for crushing

Canines for stabbing

Goat

Lion

ORIGINS OF MAMMALS

There have been mammals on earth for more than 200 million years. The first kinds appeared during the Late Triassic Period. This was the time when dinosaurs were beginning to spread and take over the land.

ONE OF THE FIRST

Tiny Megazostrodon *fossils, of 4.7 inches (12 centimeters) long, were found in South Africa. They lived 200 million years ago, at the same time as the dinosaurs (below). They hid from the dinosaurs by day and came out at night to feed on insects and grubs. (Picture not to scale)*

MAMMAL ANCESTORS

The creatures that gave rise to mammals were probably the therapsids, also called the advanced mammallike reptiles. These started as reptiles with scaly skin. Then some of them gradually changed, or evolved. Mammallike features appeared. These included fur, specialized teeth, a single bone for the lower jaw, and a new type of ear design with three tiny bones inside. The first mammals had arrived.

SIMILAR TO THE FIRST MAMMALS

Tree shrews are the mammals living today that most resemble early mammals such as the *Megazostrodon* (above right). They are not real shrews, and they have their own mammal group, the tupaids. They have long pointed snouts, large eyes, small sharp teeth, five sharp-clawed toes on each foot, and furry tails. Tree shrews live in the tropical forests of Southeast Asia. They eat small creatures like moths and bugs, as well as fruits.

Tree shrews hunt food in the trees and on the ground.

TAKING TO AIR

By 50 million years ago, some mammals' front legs had developed into wings. These mammals became bats. Icaronycteris fossils from North America show a wingspan of 16 inches (41 cm).

TAKING TO THE SEA

Some mammals adapted to water. Their front legs became flippers, and their tails became flukes. Basilosaurus, an early whale from 40 million years ago, was 82 feet (25 m) long.

MAMMAL FOSSILS

The changes from reptile to mammal can be seen from the remains of bones, teeth, and other hard body parts, preserved in rocks as fossils. The evidence of fossils shows that during the Age of Dinosaurs, between 200 million and 65 million years ago, mammals were small and scarce. Hardly any were larger than a pet cat of today.

Dinosaurs and many other bigger creatures died out in a worldwide disaster 65 million years ago. Mammals survived and soon began to rapidly evolve. Some remained small and shrewlike, feeding on worms and insects. Others became much larger and started to eat plants. By 30 million years ago, all the main mammal groups we know today had appeared.

NOT SO OLD

Since the early days of mammals, many species have appeared and died out. One of the most recent to disappear was the woolly mammoth, which became extinct less than 10,000 years ago. Some of these mammoths, such as baby Dima who was found in Siberia, are preserved in the ice.

Mammoth "Dima" was frozen as a baby.

Skin and Fur

No other animals have furry or hairy skin like mammals. However, not all mammals have a lot of fur. Some, like whales and rhinos, lost almost all of their body hair as their species evolved.

WHAT IS FUR FOR?

In the early mammals, fur or hair probably first appeared as a form of insulation. Fur keeps the cold out, so a mammal can keep its body warm all the time. Mammals that live in cold places today, such as seals in polar oceans and mountain sheep and goats, have very thick fur. A layer of hair can also keep out too much heat, so that the body does not overheat, as with camels in the desert.

HAIRLESS BUT STILL WARM

The walrus has almost no fur. But its extra-thick layer of fat under the skin, called blubber, keeps in body warmth.

PROTECTED PORCUPINE

A tree porcupine's quills are sharp, stiff, extra-long hairs. If a predator attacks, the quills come loose and stick into its flesh, working their way inward.

LONGEST HAIRS

Large mammals from very cold places, such as the musk ox of the Arctic tundra, have the longest hairs. The hairs of the outer coat are up to 3 feet (90 cm) long. Rain and snow drip off these long hairs, which keeps the thick underfur dry.

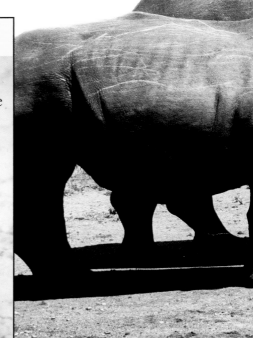

FUR AS PROTECTION

Fur or hair has other uses besides insulation. It protects soft skin from bruises and scrapes. In some mammals, such as porcupines and hedgehogs, hairs have become long, sharp spines that deter enemies. In pangolins, fur has evolved into large flat plates of tough horn that cover the skin. Armadillos have similar plates of bone covered with horn. These give even better protection.

LOOKING BIG

Hairs can be moved by small muscles attached to their roots in the skin. If the hairs are tilted to stand straight up, they trap a thicker layer of air. This helps to keep in even more body warmth. Also, as fur stands on end, it makes the mammal look bigger and stronger, which can help scare away attackers.

ENCASED IN ARMOR

The pangolin's scalelike plates of horn overlap to form a "suit of armor."

SKIN AND HAIR CARE

Some furry mammals like tamarins (above) groom themselves or each other to keep their fur clean and healthy. Without grooming, they would be covered in parasites. Some furless mammals like rhinos (below and left) wallow in wet mud. This moistens and protects their skin against pests like biting flies.

COLORS AND CAMOUFLAGE

Why are polar bears white and grizzly bears brown? Why do mandrills have colorful faces? There are several reasons for the colors of a mammal's skin and fur.

BLENDING IN

Many mammals are colored for camouflage. This means they merge or blend into their surroundings. One of the clearest examples is the polar bear. Its icy surroundings are mainly white. So the polar bear is white, too. This allows it to creep up on prey such as seals with less chance of being seen. Predators like lions that live in dry grasslands tend to be brown or tan. They match the grass stems and earth. Mammals that are hunted, from mice to deer, are also camouflaged so they are less easily seen by their predators.

BRIGHT FOR BREEDING

Mandrills are the largest monkeys. A full-grown male has a red and blue face, yellow beard, and blue rump. These colors advertise that he is mature and ready to reproduce.

DAZZLED AND CONFUSED

If a zebra is attacked, the herd stampedes. Their fast-moving striped bodies create a confusing "dazzle," making it difficult to pick out a victim.

DAPPLED TO HIDE

Young deer or fawns lie still in the forest undergrowth. The light spots on their coat match the shafts of sunlight shining through the leaves.

DAPPLED TO HUNT

Like the fawn (left), the leopard's spots help it hide as it lies under trees. It usually hides on a low branch, ready to drop onto passing prey.

STANDING OUT

Camouflage is only one reason for color. Some species of mammals want to be noticed. They have colorful patterns, especially on their faces. This is usually to attract mates at breeding time. The colors do not develop until the animal is full-grown.

WARNING!

Another reason for a mammal's colors is to warn of some kind of danger. Creatures that try to attack a skunk are sprayed with a foul-smelling, skin-irritating fluid. They soon learn to recognize the skunk's bold black-and-white pattern, which is known as warning coloration.

STAY CLEAR

The striped skunk's white stripe works as a warning signal to predators. It reminds them of the skunk's smelly spray.

CHANGING COLORS

Some habitats change greatly with the seasons. The Arctic fox lives among ice and snow in winter, but among bare earth and low plants in summer. In spring it molts, or sheds its white coat, and grows darker fur. It molts back to white in the fall.

An Arctic fox in summer (inset) and winter (right)

MAMMAL SENSES

Mammals have the same main senses as we do—since humans are mammals, too. These senses are sight, hearing, smell, taste, and touch. However, some mammals can see, hear, and especially smell much better than we can.

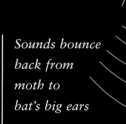

SENSES IN NOCTURNAL ANIMALS

Many mammals are nocturnal, or active at night. They usually have extra-sharp senses for this kind of lifestyle. Often, they have large eyes to see as much light as possible in the dark, big ears to pick up faint sounds, and elongated, quivering noses. Long whiskers are also important for nocturnal mammals, as they help them feel their way around in darkness.

Sounds bounce back from moth to bat's big ears

HOW BATS "SEE" BY HEARING

Bats use a method called echolocation to find their way and hunt for prey in darkness. The bat sends out very high-pitched or ultrasonic squeaks, clicks, and other noises. These bounce or reflect off nearby objects as echoes. The bat hears the pattern of returning echoes and works out the size and location of objects as small as gnats.

HEARING

All mammals can hear, but not all have outer ear flaps, or pinnae, on the sides of the head. Water-dwellers such as whales and seals lack these flaps, for better streamlining. But they still have the inner parts of the ear to detect sounds and vibrations under the surface.

In most mammals, the larger the ear flaps, the better the sense of hearing. Plant-eaters such as zebras and antelopes have large cupped ears that tilt and swivel in any direction. These ears can pick out the precise direction of a sound, such as the rustle of grass, which may signal an approaching predator.

BIG EARS

The African serval hunts mainly at dawn and dusk—and mainly by hearing. It waits silently in long grasses, listening for prey such as rats.

HUGE EYES
The slender loris has the biggest eyes, compared to its head size, of any mammal. This nocturnal primate lives in South Asian forests.

SIGHT

The size of eyes shows how much a mammal depends on them. Underground, moles have tiny eyes that hardly work. Night-active rats, bats, and monkeys have relatively big eyes for seeing in dim light.

Eye position is also important. Plant-eaters like rabbits and deer have eyes on the sides of the head. This gives them good all-round vision to watch for predators. The eyes of hunters usually face forward, which lets the animals judge distance precisely when pouncing on prey.

SMELL AND TASTE

Compared to other mammals, our sight and hearing are average—but our sense of smell is poor. In the clear Arctic air, a polar bear uses its long muzzle to sniff the scent of a dead seal from 3 miles (4.8 kilometers) away. In forests, mammals such as wild boars have long, flexible snouts. These probe in soil and sniff for food. Mammals like monkeys with flatter snouts rely less on smell and more on sight. Most mammals use their sense of taste to check if food is suitable to eat. In general, they avoid bitter flavors.

LONG NOSE
The elephant shrew (which is not a true shrew) is named after its long, trunklike snout.

A STRANGE SENSE

The platypus of eastern Australia has an "extra sense." In water, its leathery beaklike muzzle can detect tiny pulses of electricity, which are given off naturally by the muscles of moving creatures. (These electrical signals do not travel through air, so this sense is limited to watery habitats.) The platypus noses in riverbed mud to sense its food of worms, shellfish, and water insects.

The platypus' "duck bill" can sense electricity.

HOW MAMMALS MOVE

Mammals move on land, in water, in air, and even through soil. The basic body design with four legs and a tail varies greatly depending on the main method of movement—from walking, leaping, hopping, and running to swimming and flying.

LEAPING TO SAFETY
Bush babies use their rear legs to leap 16.5 feet (5 m).

LEGS FOR SPEED AND POWER

Mammals with long slim legs, such as deer, antelopes, and horses, are usually fast movers. These are ungulates, or hoofed mammals. Their running muscles are mostly in the shoulder and thigh regions, rather than spread along the legs. Combined with strong yet lightweight hooves, this means that the long legs can swing back and forth very rapidly with very little effort.

Some mammals, like rabbits, hares, kangaroo rats, gerbils, and kangaroos, have much larger rear legs than front ones. These mammals use their powerful back legs to hop or leap.

Larger mammals such as elephants, rhinos, and hippos put strength before speed. They have powerful, thick legs to carry their heavy bodies. Yet many of them can sprint surprisingly fast. A rhino charges at more than 31 miles (50 km) per hour, much faster than any human runner.

FASTEST SPRINTER

The fastest mammal is the cheetah. It can reach speeds of more than 62 miles (99 km) per hour—but only for half a minute. Then it must rest. The cheetah has long legs and a very flexible back. As it sprints, its back arches up and down. This allows its legs to swing through a wide arc and cover a great distance with each stride.

Back arches up; legs almost overlap

Back arches down; legs fully extend

SHOVELS FOR PAWS

A mole's network of tunnels may be more than 220 yards (200 m) long. It digs using its short, muscular forelimbs and wide, blunt claws. It can displace twice its own weight of dirt in a minute.

CLIMBERS AND DIGGERS

Two specialized habitats for movement are trees and soil. Arboreal (tree-living) mammals have flexible limbs with sharp claws or grasping fingers to grip the bark. Moles, aardvarks, wombats, and other diggers have wide shovellike paws.

SWINGING AWAY

The gibbons of Southeast Asia move by a method called brachiation. They swing through the branches by their arms, hanging from their hooklike hands. As the gibbon moves, it builds up a back-and-forth motion, like a pendulum. This helps the animal save energy.

FULL GALLOP

Zebras can gallop at more than 40 miles (64 km) per hour and kick out with their sharp hooves in defense.

SLOWEST MAMMAL

In a typical day, a sloth travels a total distance of less than 55 yards (50 m). This Central and South American tree-dweller has the slowest natural gait of any mammal. It often takes a minute to move just a few feet.

A sloth taking it easy

SWIMMING AND FLYING

Mammals have mastered every habitat, including the skies and seas. Movement through air or water requires different limbs from movement on land. The limb design must include a large surface for pushing against the air or water. Such limbs are called wings or flippers.

SWIMMING

Part-time swimmers such as otters can also travel on land. So their limbs are similar to both flippers and paws. The foot is broad with webs of skin between the toes, which makes a wide surface for pushing against water. Yet the toes still have claws and can grip well even in soft mud.

Other mammals, such as seals and sea lions, are ideally suited to moving in water. These mammals have paddlelike limbs and are clumsy on land. Fully aquatic (water-living) mammals like whales, dolphins, and sea cows (manatees and dugongs) do not need gripping toes. Their limbs are broad flippers that can row or flap. These mammals get their main swimming power from their backbones.

TAIL FLAP

The manatee has flipper-shaped front limbs and a broad, rounded tail. It is a peaceful plant-eater.

DUAL-PURPOSE DESIGN

The otter moves well on land and in water, where it kicks hard with its webbed feet.

BIG PADDLES

The polar bear's enormous paws work well as wide paddles for swimming and also as snowshoes to stop it from sinking in snow.

Sea lions (far left) swim with the front flippers, flapping to "fly" through the water. Seals (left) use their rear flippers for power and front ones for steering. Humpback whales (main) have the longest flippers of all mammals at 13 feet (4 m).

FLYING AND GLIDING

Of all the species, or kinds, of mammals, about one-fourth can truly fly. They are bats. Their front limbs are wings made of very thin leathery skin, mainly stretched across the bones of the second and fifth fingers. "Flying" squirrels and "flying" lemurs, or colugos, are really gliders. They cannot stay in the air for long, although they have good steering control.

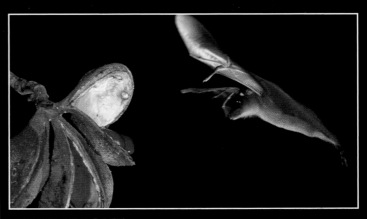

GLIDING SQUIRREL

The flying squirrel has large flaps of furry skin along its sides and steers with its tail.

FLUKE POWER

Whales and dolphins have flipper-like front limbs—but no rear limbs. The tail flaps, or flukes, are muscle and skin, with no bones. Power comes from arching the back to swish the flukes up and down.

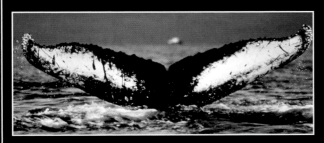

A humpback's flukes have wavy rear edges.

TRUE FLIGHT

A bat uses chest and shoulder muscles to flap its wings. Some kinds can hover or fly backward.

MAMMAL COMMUNICATION

Few animals communicate as much as mammals, who do so not only with other creatures, but also with their own kind. Mammals use many ways to send their messages, including sights, sounds, and scents.

WHY COMMUNICATE?
Compared to the rest of the animal kingdom, mammals have complicated behavior. Communication, which is part of this behavior, is often used for survival. For example, a mammal in danger uses sights, sounds, and smells. It fluffs up its fur to look bigger and faces the attacker while showing its teeth, claws, or other weapons. It makes a menacing sound, and may give off an unpleasant scent.

Each method of communication has advantages. Sights and sounds work at once and over reasonable distances, but are then gone. Smells usually take longer to produce, but they also last longer and can act across even greater distances.

STRIPES AND SMELLS
The ring-tailed lemur smears its scent on its tail and waves it like a flag.

DAWN MESSAGE
The howler monkey's early morning whoops tell other howler monkeys, "This part of the forest is mine. Keep out!"

USEFUL HOWLS
Coyotes seem to howl at the moon. They are really keeping in touch with their partner or group members, and warning other coyotes to stay away.

TERRITORIAL MARKING

Some mammals have territories—areas where they live and feed—that they defend against others. Territories are marked in various ways, such as by urine and droppings. The smelly signals last for days and mean, "This territory is taken."

A male rhino sprays urine around its territory.

Tigers leave scratch marks.

SMILING OR SCARED?

Monkeys and apes make many kinds of facial expressions that do not always correspond with our own. If a chimp "smiles," it is really afraid.

TOO LOW FOR US TO HEAR

Some mammals send messages that we cannot hear. Elephants communicate by very low-pitched rumbles that travel well over the land.

WITHIN THE GROUP

Many mammals that live in groups communicate by sending messages to others in their family, herd, pack, or troop. These messages may involve the location of food, warnings of predators or other dangers, being ready to mate at breeding time, or contests for leadership of the group.

MEAT-EATERS

The main tools of a meat-eating mammal are sharp teeth and claws, as well as sharp senses. These traits depend on the type of prey being hunted.

BIG AND SMALL PREY

Meat-eaters that hunt sizeable victims are usually called predators. They include a wide range of mammals, from weasels and otters, to cats big and small, to dolphins and seals in the sea. Some mammals, like jackals and hyenas, also eat the carcasses of dead creatures and are known as scavengers.

Certain smaller mammals specialize in tiny prey such as insects, spiders, worms, and grubs. They are known by the general name of insectivores. They include shrews, hedgehogs, moles, moonrats (gymnures), tenrecs, and solenodons.

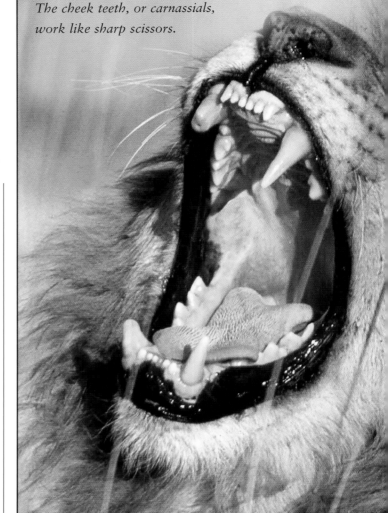

PREDATOR TEETH

Most mammal hunters, such as lions, have small front incisor teeth but very long fangs, or canines. These are for jabbing into and ripping up prey. The cheek teeth, or carnassials, work like sharp scissors.

CATS AND DOGS

Most cats (apart from lions and cheetahs) hunt alone, like the tiger. Most dogs, like African wild dogs (right), cooperate in groups called packs.

TRAPPING PREY

Though great whales are meat-eaters, they lack teeth. Instead, they have fringed baleen plates hanging from the upper jaw. The baleen works like a strainer. The whale gulps in water full of tiny shrimplike krill. It pushes the water back out through the baleen, trapping krill inside.

LONG AND SLIM

Mustelids like weasels have slim, flexible bodies, which are ideal for wriggling down burrows after prey.

ALL TYPES OF CARNIVORES

The term *carnivore* means "flesh-eater." Carnivores belong to a mammal group called the Carnivora. This includes a range of predators from wolves, wild dogs, and foxes to mustelids, civets, and linsangs, as well as mongooses, raccoons and coatis, hyenas, and all cats—a total of about 250 species.

Bears are included in the Carnivora group. They have the large stabbing teeth, called canines, of a typical meat-eater. Sometimes they hunt large prey. But most bears, apart from the polar bear, eat more plant foods than meat. One of them, the giant panda, eats almost no meat at all.

BIGGEST PREDATOR

The sperm whale is by far the world's biggest predator. It grows to 22 yards (20 m) long and weighs about 50 tons (45 metric tons). Its main prey are octopus, fish, and squid.

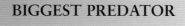

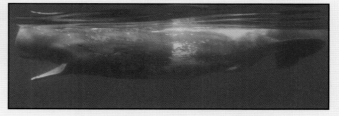

A sperm whale rests before its hunting dive.

SMALLEST PREDATOR

Tiny shrews are fierce hunters and tackle prey as big as themselves.

PLANT-EATERS

More than half of mammals are plant-eaters. Together, they munch almost every part of a plant, from roots to grasses, bark, sap, leaves, buds, flowers, and fruits.

BIGGER MEALS

Compared to meat, plant foods are harder to chew, more difficult to digest, and contain fewer nutrients. So the plant-eating mammals, or herbivores, have to spend much more time eating than the carnivores. A typical herbivore has wide, flat-topped cheek teeth, or molars, for crushing its food. It also usually has long jaws and powerful jaw muscles. Rats, voles, and other rodents have long, chisellike front teeth for nibbling and gnawing.

GREAT GRAZERS

Grass leaves and stems have hard, tiny grains that make them difficult to crush to a pulp. Bison spend up to 20 hours each day chewing.

GREAT BROWSERS

The giraffe (below left) can extend its tongue 18 inches (46 cm) to wrap around leaves. An elephant (below) eats about 330 pounds (148.5 kilograms) of food a day.

MIDNIGHT APPETITE

Like its huge, river-dwelling cousin, the forest-loving pygmy hippo feeds under cover of darkness. It eats a wider variety of foods than the hippo, including mosses, ferns, twigs, and fruits.

SAME MEAL EVERY DAY

Only a few herbivores have limited diets. In Australia, the koala (below left) prefers the leaves of just a few eucalyptus or gum trees. In China, the giant panda (below right) eats mainly bamboo, but it also snacks on grubs, birds' eggs, and even carrion (dead animals).

SPECIALIST HERBIVORES

Grazers eat mainly grasses and include zebras, hippos, and several kinds of deer. Browsers, such as giraffes and camels, tend to feed on bushes and trees. Some larger hoofed herbivores swallow food into the first part of the stomach. They bring it back up later to munch some more, or "chew the cud," before swallowing it again. This is necessary because grasses are hard to digest. These ruminants include deer, antelopes, camels, giraffes, and cattle.

ALL FULL

After a big meal of leaves and fruits, the proboscis monkey's full stomach makes up half of its total weight.

MIGRATE OR HIBERNATE?

Some regions have a very harsh time of year, like a freezing winter or a seasonal drought. Mammals have two options—stay put and sleep, or move away to better conditions.

THERE AND BACK AGAIN

Most migrations are regular long journeys to and from the same place, at the same time each year. Conditions that cause mammals to migrate include lack of food, great cold or heat, or a long dry period. In North America, caribou travel south in autumn, leaving the frozen Arctic tundra for the shelter of the northern forests in winter. The next spring they trek north again for the brief summer when the tundra supports plentiful plant life.

Some mammals migrate in a more random way. On the dry, cold steppes (grasslands) of Central Asia, saiga antelope wander with the varied pattern of rains, which bring fresh plant growth.

DANGERS OF MIGRATION

Long journeys bring many dangers. In Africa, as wildebeest cross a river, they are at risk from drowning, being trampled, and being attacked by crocodiles.

SHALLOW TO DEEP

Some porpoises migrate between deeper waters and coastal shallows, following groups of prey.

GRAY WHALE MIGRATION

The greatest mammal migrants are gray whales. Each spring they cruise to the Arctic, where extra warmth means food is plentiful. In fall, they swim south to subtropical coasts. Some gray whales journey 12,000 miles (19,200 km) each year.

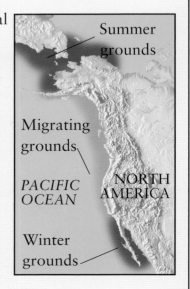

Summer grounds

Migrating grounds

PACIFIC OCEAN

NORTH AMERICA

Winter grounds

Bears sleep for up to six months, but not as deeply as true hibernators. This is called dormancy. They may wake up and leave the den in mild weather.

WINTER SLEEP

An alternative to migration is hibernation, or extra-deep sleep through the coldest months. This saves energy when food is most scarce. The main hibernators are various types of bats and rodents such as jerboas, squirrels, and woodchucks. Birch mice and alpine marmots may spend eight months asleep. The body temperature of deep hibernators like dormice and bats falls from almost 104 degrees Fahrenheit (40 degrees Celsius) to 41 F (5 C) or less, with one breath or heartbeat every few minutes.

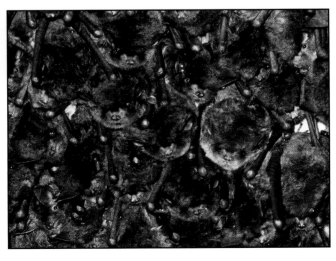

CURLED DORMICE

Hibernating mammals feed well in autumn and store food as body fat. When these dormice (above) wake in spring, they will have lost up to one-third of their body weight.

CLUSTERED BATS

Bats gather (right) at a regular site called a hibernaculum, such as a cave. Clustered together, they are safer from enemies and freezing weather.

33

NESTS AND DENS

Most mammals have some kind of home. This gives them a safe place to rest, eat food, and also store it. Often this nest or den is the place to rear a family, too.

BUILDERS
The most elaborate mammal home is the beaver's lodge. It is a large, strong dome up to 11 yards (10 m) wide, built of sticks, stones, and mud. It is in a lake or pool and has underwater entrances to keep out enemies such as wolves. Often the beavers dam a nearby stream to create the lake. Muskrats may also build a lodge-type dwelling, although less complicated than the beaver's. On land, some mammals build homes by walking around or rolling over an area of forest undergrowth, flattening it into a simple nest.

UPKEEP
Burrow-nesters like meerkats spend up to an hour each day keeping their homes clean and repaired. Few predators can enter—except snakes.

BEAVERS AT WORK

The whole beaver family, including the young or kits, gnaw branches and twigs from trees to build and maintain the lodge.

A fox's underground den is known as an earth, and it may be used year after year.

The harvest mouse builds an intricate small nest the size and shape of a tennis ball. The nest is made of stems and leaves woven onto long grasses. Its single entrance is a thumbnail-sized hole.

Harvest mouse nest

BURROWERS

The most common types of mammal homes are burrows or tunnels in the earth. The largest, dug by wombats and aardvarks, have entrances of up to 3 feet (90 cm) wide. A European badger's family burrow system, called a sett, may have 220 yards (200 m) of underground passages and more than 10 entrances. Many rodents such as gerbils and mole rats also have burrow homes. Most of them dig their own, but some take over or enlarge an old burrow, as when a fox family moves into a rabbit warren.

MAKING THE BED

Apes, such as the orangutan, weave branches to make a rough sleeping platform of twigs and leaves. They build a new nest this way each evening.

READY TO BREED

Breeding, or reproduction, is a key feature of all animal life, and mammals have some of the most fascinating methods. The first step is to get a male and female together.

PARTNER CHECK

Unlike certain creatures, such as worms and snails, every mammal is either male or female. Males and females must come together to mate before offspring are produced. Often there is a series of specific actions and behaviors before mating, which is known as courtship.

Courtship allows each partner to make sure that the other one is fit, healthy, fully grown, in breeding condition, and of the same species. Partners of different species cannot produce healthy offspring, which wastes the vital chance to breed.

SHOWING OFF

Male deer gather to do battle for females during the rutting season.

LOVE SONGS IN THE SEA

Courtship sounds are very common, from simple squeaks or grunts to the amazing "songs" of the great whales. The male humpback sings a complex series of notes lasting 30 minutes or more—all day and all night, too. His eerie wails and moans travel hundreds of miles through the ocean.

A humpback hangs head-down as he sings.

WHO'S BOSS?
Male elephant seals rear up, roar, and bite each other. The winner mates with 100 or more females.

BATTLE TO BREED

In some mammals, such as cats, a single male and female pair carries out courtship by themselves. They may attract each other over long distances by scents and sounds.

In other mammals, members of one sex, nearly always males, gather at breeding time and battle for the opportunity to mate. The males make threatening sounds and show off to each other, perhaps by pushing and shoving. In most cases these battles are "ritualized." The actions follow a set pattern, and the loser gives in before getting hurt. But in a few species, the contests are more dangerous, and males are wounded or even killed. Often the winner mates with many females.

FIGHTING OR COURTING?

A male and a female kangaroo may jab each other with their paws when courting.

BANGING HEADS

Male sheep, goats (below), and gazelles (inset) have pushing contests to see which is strongest and who will produce strong offspring.

BIRTH AND BABIES

Most animals lay eggs, but the vast majority of mammals give birth to babies. They all feed their young on mother's milk.

HOW MANY BABIES?

The number of babies born at one time is called litter size. Some mammals have large litters of 20 or more. But their babies are small and helpless, and must be kept warm and safe for a long time, usually in a nest. Rats, mice, and other rodents have these types of litters, as do cats and dogs.

Other mammal mothers have just one or two babies each time. These offspring are usually well-developed and able to look after themselves, although they still need their mother's milk. The main examples are whales, seals, and hoofed mammals, such as rhinos, cattle, and zebras.

NO BABYSITTER

The young tapir (above) and seal (inset) are left on their own while their mothers feed. Their camouflage keeps them hidden and safe from predators while their mothers are away.

A LARGE LITTER

The garden dormouse has big litters so at least a few babies survive frequent attacks by predators.

A SAFE DEN

Predators like wolves (right) leave their offspring in a den while out hunting.

A DANGEROUS TIME

Most mammal mothers hide in a burrow, nest, or another quiet place to give birth. On the open plains, large mammals cannot do this. So their offspring are born well-developed. The sights and especially the smells of birth soon attract predators. Within a few minutes the newborn can walk and then run with the herd.

A wildebeest calf is ready to run in minutes.

CARING PARENTS

Mammal parents provide more care for their offspring than any other creatures except birds. In most cases, the mother carries out this care. She keeps a lookout for danger, protects her babies against predators, and feeds them milk made in her mammary glands.

After a time, the offspring start to become more independent. They stop drinking milk and begin to eat other foods. This stage is called weaning. Some mice are weaned at less than two weeks old. Otters are weaned at eight weeks, most great whales at six months, and young chimps and elephants at three or four years.

A FATHER'S TOUCH

Only a small number of mammal fathers take part in rearing their young. They include wolves and foxes, and also small monkeys called marmosets (above) and tamarins.

POUCHES AND EGGS

In about 7 percent of mammals, the babies grow in a pocketlike pouch on the mother's front, called the marsupium. So these mammals are known as marsupials. Three species of mammals do not give birth to babies, but lay eggs. They are called monotremes.

WHERE MARSUPIALS LIVE

South America has about 100 marsupial species, mainly tree-dwellers such as opossums. Only one kind, the Virginia opossum, occurs in the United States. All other marsupials live in Australia and New Guinea. Long ago, they had no competition from other mammals in Australia. So Australia has marsupial versions of many other mammals, such as marsupial moles, shrews, and cats.

KOALA

The koala is the marsupial equivalent of a small bear. It lives and feeds in eucalyptus trees, rarely coming to the ground.

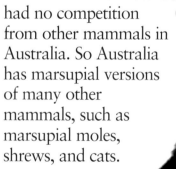

KANGAROO

Kangaroos eat the sparse plants of the Australian outback. The baby, called a joey, begins to leave the pouch at six months old and is independent by a year.

TASMANIAN DEVIL

The Tasmanian devil is a smallish, doglike hunter-scavenger. The babies stay in their mother's pouch for about 15 weeks.

VIRGINIA OPOSSUM

This marsupial (above right) has large litters with five to 13 young—and occasionally more than 30. It is slowly spreading its range in North America.

MARSUPIAL BREEDING

Newborn marsupial babies are far smaller, compared to their mothers, than babies of other mammals. The largest marsupial, the red kangaroo, is as tall as a person. Yet its newborn is even smaller than your little finger. It is born bald and undeveloped.

Its eyes and ears are closed, and its legs are like tiny flaps. It crawls to its mother's pouch to feed on her milk, and continues to grow. Most marsupials spend their first weeks like this. As the young grow, the mother leaves them in a den or "parks" them on a branch as she forages for food.

EGG-LAYING MAMMALS

Mammal babies hatched from eggs still feed on milk like other mammals. These egg-laying mammals, or monotremes, are the platypus of eastern Australia and two kinds of echidnas, or spiny anteaters, in Australia and New Guinea. The one or two eggs of the platypus hatch after 10 days, and the mother feeds the babies for up to a month. The long-nosed echidna carries her newly hatched babies in a pouch, like a marsupial.

The young are reared by their mother in a nest burrow.

SAVING MAMMALS

The world seems full of familiar mammals such as dogs, sheep, and cattle. But in the wild, one mammal species in five is in danger. The hazards they face are usually caused by the most numerous and most dominant mammal of all—humans.

THREATS EVERYWHERE

The greatest overall danger facing mammals (and all other animals) is habitat loss. This is the disappearance of their natural homes and wild places, taken over for farms, houses, planted forests, roads, parks, factories, and other uses. Some species are affected by pollution or captured alive as exotic pets. Others are hunted for trophies, souvenirs, or "sport," or because they threaten farm animals and people. Some are killed for their meat.

HABITAT LOSS

Most mammals, like orangutans, live in tropical forests. These habitats are quickly being destroyed to harvest timber and make way for crops and pasture for farm animals.

DANGERS AT SEA

Marine mammals such as seals and dolphins drown in vast nets meant for fish. Large-scale whaling ceased in the 1980s, but some nations say whale numbers have now recovered and wish to resume the hunt.

HOW WE ARE HELPING

International laws prevent the killing of hundreds of mammal species. The Convention on International Trade in Endangered Species (CITES) prevents selling their body parts or products. In captivity, mammals are bred in zoos or parks, and as their numbers build, they are released back into the wild.

Publicity campaigns help rare mammals such as gorillas, tigers, and rhinos. But the main need of all mammals is a natural, safe place to live. If habitat loss is the biggest threat, then habitat preservation is the greatest solution to saving mammals.

SOUVENIRS

Despite regulations, people still offer items for sale made from lawfully protected species.

BUSH MEAT

The bush meat trade involves hunting mammals in the wild, even gorillas (above), and selling their meat at local markets (right). It is a growing threat, especially in Africa.

ANIMAL CLASSIFICATION

The animal kingdom can be split into two main groups, vertebrates (with a backbone) and invertebrates (without a backbone). From these two main groups, scientists classify, or sort, animals further based on their shared characteristics.

The six main groupings of animals, from the most general to the most specific, are: phylum, class, order, family, genus, and species. This system was created by Carolus Linnaeus.

To see how this system works, follow the example of how human beings are classified in the vertebrate group and how earthworms are classified in the invertebrate group.

ANIMAL KINGDOM

VERTEBRATE

PHYLUM: Chordata

CLASS: Mammals

ORDER: Primates

FAMILY: Hominids

GENUS: *Homo*

SPECIES: *sapiens*

INVERTEBRATE

PHYLUM: Annelida

CLASS: Oligochaeta

ORDER: Haplotaxida

FAMILY: Lumbricidae

GENUS: *Lumbricus*

SPECIES: *terrestris*

There are more than 30 groups of phyla. The nine most common are listed below along with their common name.

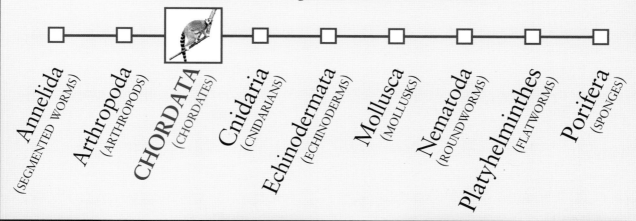

Annelida
(SEGMENTED WORMS)

Arthropoda
(ARTHROPODS)

CHORDATA
(CHORDATES)

Cnidaria
(CNIDARIANS)

Echinodermata
(ECHINODERMS)

Mollusca
(MOLLUSKS)

Nematoda
(ROUNDWORMS)

Platyhelminthes
(FLATWORMS)

Porifera
(SPONGES)

This book highlights animals from the Chordata phylum. Follow the example below to learn how scientists classify the *giganteus*, or eastern grey kangaroo.

VERTEBRATE

PHYLUM: Chordata

CLASS: Mammalia

ORDER: Diprotodontia

FAMILY: Macropodidae

GENUS: *Macropus*

SPECIES: *giganteus*

Eastern grey kangaroo (giganteus)

GLOSSARY

AQUATIC
Living only or mostly in water, like whales, dolphins, porpoises, seals, sea lions, and manatees

ARBOREAL
Living mainly in trees, like most kinds of monkeys

BLUBBER
In mammals such as seals and whales, a thick layer of fat just under the skin that keeps in body warmth

BROWSER
An animal that eats leaves and other plant parts in bushes and trees, rather than low-growing plants on the ground

CAMOUFLAGE
The disguising of an animal by the way it is colored and patterned to blend or merge with its surroundings; shape and scent can also be used for camouflage

CANINES
Long, sharp teeth near the front of the mouth for stabbing and jabbing

CARNIVORE
An animal that eats mainly other creatures, especially their flesh or meat

COLD-BLOODED
Having a body temperature that varies with the temperature of the surroundings, so an animal is cool in cold weather and warm in hot sunny weather

EVOLUTION
The change in living things through time as they become better adapted or suited to their surroundings or environment

FLUKES
The broad surfaces or "tail" of whales, dolphins, and porpoises

GRAZER
An animal that eats mainly grasses and similar low-growing plants

HABITAT
A particular type of surroundings or environment where plants and animals live, such as a desert, mountainside, pond, or seashore

HERBIVORE
An animal that eats mainly plant parts, including leaves, stems, shoots, fruits, and seeds

HIBERNATION
A special kind of very deep sleep, when a warm-blooded animal's body processes slow down and it becomes cold and inactive, usually to save energy during a cold period

INCISORS
Sharp-edged teeth at the front of the mouth for nibbling and gnawing

MAMMARY GLANDS
Internal organs on the front of a female mammal's body, which make milk to feed her young

MARSUPIUM
The pocketlike pouch on the front of a female marsupial mammal, where the babies continue to develop after birth

MIGRATION
A regular long journey by an animal, usually at the same time each year, to avoid harsh conditions such as cold or drought

NOCTURNAL
Active at night, usually to feed or move from place to place

RUMINANT
A mammal that swallows food, then brings it back up to chew again (called "chewing the cud"), and swallows it once more, to get more nutrients from it

SUCKLE
To feed a baby mammal milk from the mother's mammary glands

TERRESTRIAL
Living mainly on land or on the ground, like mammals that dwell in deserts, grasslands, and mountains

TERRITORY
An area where a mammal lives, and which it defends against others of its kind; some territories are used only for feeding, some for breeding, and some for both

WARM-BLOODED
Using the energy in food to keep the body at a constant warm temperature at all times, even if the temperature of the surroundings varies greatly; the main groups of warm-blooded animals are mammals and birds

WOMB
Part of the body of a female mammal where her babies develop before they are born; also called the uterus

FURTHER RESOURCES

AT THE LIBRARY
Dalgleish, Sharon. *Mighty Mammals*. Broomall, Penn.: Mason Crest Publishers, 2003.

Parker, Steve. *Mammal*. New York: Dorling Kindersely, 2004.

Spilsbury, Louise and Richard. *Classification: From Mammals to Fungi*. Chicago: Heinemann Library, 2004.

Turner, Alan. *National Geographic Prehistoric Mammals*. Washington, D.C.: National Geographic, 2004.

ON THE WEB
For more information on this topic, use FactHound.
1. Go to *www.facthound.com*
2. Type in this book ID: 0756512530
3. Click on the *Fetch It* button.
FactHound will find the best Web sites for you.

INDEX